Ernest George Gets a Home

Jill Eileen

Fulton Books
Meadville, PA

Published by Fulton Books 2023

ISBN 979-8-88982-421-3 (paperback)
ISBN 979-8-88982-422-0 (digital)

Printed in the United States of America

To the real-life Jessy (Jesbir K. Singh). Without her heroic acts, I would not have my real-life Ernest George. Not to mention Eloise LaRue and Daphne Michelle too. Not only do I treasure these house lions but the sisterhood that rescuing Ernest George sparked between us is a bond that will never be broken. Sisters forever!

Once upon a time, in a small town, there lived a little girl named Jessy. Jessy loved animals and dreamed of having a pet of her own.

One day, while walking home from school, Jessy heard a faint meowing coming from an alley. When she went to investigate, she found a small scruffy-looking kitten huddled in a corner of a box.

Jessy quickly realized that he was in bad shape. He had cuts and bruises all over his body, and his fur was matted and dirty. Jessy knew she had to help him, so she gently picked him up and brought him home.

At home, Jessy cleaned the kitten up and gave him a warm meal. She named him Ernest George after her favorite book character. Despite his injuries, Ernest George was a friendly and affectionate kitten. Jessy quickly grew attached to him and wanted to keep him, but her parents wouldn't let her. Instead, they agreed to let her foster him until he was healthy enough to find his forever home.

Over the next few weeks, Jessy worked hard to nurse Ernest George back to health. She took him to the vet, gave him medicine, and made sure he got plenty of rest. As he got better, Ernest George's personality began to shine through. He was playful and loving, and he loved to cuddle.

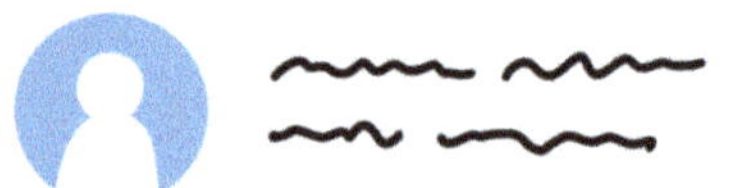

Finally, the day came when Ernest George was ready to find his forever home. Jessy was sad to say goodbye, but she knew that Ernest George deserved a loving family that would take care of him forever. She posted his story on social media, and soon a family reached out to adopt him.

The family was perfect for Ernest George. They had a big house to be filled with cat trees and toys. They also had a young son who loved animals. When Ernest George met the family, he immediately purred and rubbed against their legs as if to say, "I want to live here forever."

Ernest George's new family promised to love and take care of him always. Jessy was thrilled that she was able to give Ernest George a second chance at life. She knew that he would be happy and loved for the rest of his days.

Meeting Ernest George was the beginning of a passion for Jessy. From that day on, Jessy continued to rescue and foster animals in need. She knew that every animal deserved a chance to be loved and cared for just like Ernest George.

The End

Epilogue

Meet the real-life Ernest George. This story was inspired by his actual rescue. While his situation was much sadder than this book describes, rest assured that Ernest George is now living his best life and is spoiled rotten by the author and her family. He is believed to be part Maine coon and part Pixie-bob. He is a very loving, playful, and smart boy who rules the household (including his house lion siblings).

About the Author

Jill is a lover of all animals and volunteers at the local (currently the nation's largest) no-kill shelter. She is a full-time health tech professional who loves music, dancing, and roller skating when she isn't attending a local NHL or NFL game. Her love and passion for her fur family members since her youth ignited a passion in her to create awareness of animal rescue, foster, and forever home placement based on her personal experiences of adopting rescues into her family. Jill and her family call Las Vegas, Nevada, home.